Enemy oi
Great

By Kurt Reece-Peeplez

Good Is The Enemy Of Great

Good Is the Enemy of Great

By Kurt Reece-Peeplez

Young Excited Solz Publishing
A Division of Remnant Outreach Ministries
Mesa, AZ U.S.A.

KurtRP@KurtRP.com

Check out other books by the author at

www.KurtRP.com

Good Is The Enemy Of Great

Published by:
Young Excited Solz Publishing
Mesa, AZ U.S.A.

KurtRP.com

ISBN Paperback: 978-0-9771195-4-7
ISBN Kindle: 978-0-9771195-7-8

Library of Congress Control Number: 2017917090

Unattributed quotations are by Kurt Reece-Peeplez.

Printed in the United States of America

"This is a very motivational journey to take anyone, or any age, on. Terms used in this book can relate to a juvenile in elementary school up to a retired person. The concepts are described clearly, examples are provided and a roadmap is given for those willing to take their journey from good to greatness. This roadmap can be used with youth groups, athletic organizations, individuals, companies, literally for everyone in every facet of life.

I DON'T WANT TO SUCK!! Thanks for re-energizing me and reminding me of what everyone is capable of... GREATNESS. "

Mike Schmenger – IT Professional

"I think the whole concept of what you're writing. It applies to sports and everyday life. I like that you use it in different ways and examples far as sports, relationships, work and etc. This can apply to everyone and I think at some point we feel we have done enough when there is more that can be done. My favorite quote was when you stated when we use the word enough it sounds more could be done. That's so true! I had to sit and really think about that after I read that sentence.

Also, the levels of which you state about Good, Better, Best, and Great are on point. I think there is no way to go from Good to Great without hitting all those levels first. Then once you are great, staying there and working hard to greatness."

Clint Floyd – Professional Athlete

Table of Contents

About the Author

Kurt Reece-Peeplez is the Founder and President of The Solz Group which helps business owners overcome obstacles and reach new heights of personal and professional success. He is a business coach, youth sports coach, and entrepreneur who is dedicated to his family and looks to God to bless him so he can be a blessing to those around him.

Foreword

Awesome, Amazing and Unbelievable.

I'm dedicating this book to my son, Kalim because he is on a path and has a desire to accomplish something great. My working with him helped me forge ideas into concepts and this is what I'm sharing with you today.

His greatness will be in how he uses football to increase his platform to reach people that others can't and to create his own sphere of influence so he can, like Tim Tebow, share the good news about Jesus on a grand scale.

He is applying the concepts found in this book and it's working in helping him reach his goal of playing college. He's getting better and better academically and in football and is starting to maintain consistency in his personal growth. He is still learning many things and has a great support system in place. There is no way he can't be great and there's no way you can't be great either.

I want to thank my inner circle for their love, support and creative and constructive ideas that helped me complete this book. I also want to thank my daughters, who inspire me to be great.

I want to give special thanks to Clint Floyd for being a friend and mentor to my son and also my good friend Mike Schmenger for the encouragement and support he's given me in the time that we have known each other. Mike has been one of the greatest guys I have ever worked with.

Enjoy the book. I wrote it especially for you.

From the Author... Thank you for taking this journey with me. If you enjoyed this book, please go to Amazon and write your honest review. I would love your feedback on how you or someone you love were helped in their journey to Happiness.

Submit your review here

Good Is The Enemy Of Great

Good Is Bad

"Accepting good as a suitable level of achievement prevents you from reaching personal bests and greatness. It will impact your future."

Good in the context of this book is not in relation to evil, as in good vs bad. I use it as a measure of your effort, quality of results and consistency as it relates to what you are truly capable of in reaching your full potential.

The word potential is a powerful word that carries very deep, impactful meanings. Dictionary.com describes potential first as an adjective, then as a noun.

> adj. - having or showing the capacity to become or develop into something in the future.

> noun. - latent qualities or abilities that may be developed and lead to future success or usefulness.

It all points to future success or failure and the level of said successes of failures. You could be somewhat successful or a great success. The same goes with failure. I want you to be highly successful and great in all you do and the goal here is to help you minimize failure and maximize success.

I want you to understand that your actions are in the present and you'll realize the results of your actions in the future. The level of effort and quality of your results today, in every area of your life, affects your future in some way for good or bad. Potential is a way of measuring opportunity and how close you are to achieving your best results.

So why are we talking about potential? The title of this chapter is "Good is Bad." What does potential have to do with good being bad?

It's very simple. You will never reach your full potential if you are satisfied with good results and good results are certainly not the best results you've ever had, are they? The best result you've achieved so far in life could probably be better and realized more often with additional training, guidance, practice, dedication, and consistency. Doing these activities will allow you to continually reach higher levels of greatness and taking this approach will lead you to reach or get very close to your full potential.

Every marriage, business, employer, employee, student, teacher and athlete has potential to be more than good and achieve greatness.

Most importantly each one of you has the potential to be more than good and achieve greatness in several areas of your life. This applies to everyone, in every circumstance.

Are you starting to follow that good is not really good when it comes to reaching your full potential? Let's examine how good can be bad for you.

In what way is good bad? Good can be bad if it keeps you from accomplishing something better. We many times allow good results to stop us from achieving something greater. If this is a regular occurrence in your life, good is your enemy.

An enemy opposes you and attempts to keep you from achieving something important to you. That makes your enemy bad. It works the same way with good results.

Most people settle for good and stop trying to improve in different areas of their lives. Men and women settle below their desired mate all the time. They date or marry this "good enough" person in the hopes that they will be able to change them over time into a better version of who that person currently is.

We settle for jobs, employees, contracts, raises, and prices that are "good enough". In many cases, we could have gotten a better deal, price, raise or have found a better employee if we hadn't settled for the minimum requirements.

In school, we may settle for a B or a C, instead of continuing to work toward an A because to not fail or to pass is good enough.

Our "good enough" is equivalent to receiving that same C or less, when we desire and are capable of achieving so much more. Ask yourself, why do I settle for that C? Is it my lack of motivation, my self-esteem? Do I feel worthy or do I not really care? Everyone at some time in their life has said, "that's good enough."

The truth is, "good enough" isn't always good enough. In many cases, accepting good as a suitable level of achievement prevents you from reaching a personal best or greatness and it impacts your future. This is when good becomes bad. When you consistently do this, you allow it to become your enemy.

You are essentially surrendering to good by stopping and giving up on achieving something greater, a better marriage, a better job, better sports performance or better life.

Sometimes good is good enough, but in relationships, marriage, business, sports and other areas, it is not. A good business can be put out of business by a better one, not to mention a great one. A good marriage can withstand some trials, but a better one can withstand more. A good football player might make Varsity, but he won't start ahead of a better or great player and may never get on the field if he doesn't reach his full potential.

Even with this understanding, most people will continue to settle for "this is good enough." The word enough invokes the thought of stopping something before it is finished. "That's enough." Doesn't that sound like more could be done, a better or greater result could have been accomplished?

Pay Attention To Where You Say "That's Enough". Chances are that there is opportunity to be better than that.

Now in some cases, good enough is fine. If I'm filling my dog's water bowl and it's almost full, then yes, that is good enough, but your advancement is worth far more than how you provide water to a dog.

In this book, we explore the concept of how to go from good to great. We'll get more into it in the following chapters and it goes like this:

Good → Better1 → **Best** → Better2 → **Great**

Let me ask you, are you satisfied with what you have or still desire to accomplish in life? Are the things in your life and what you want to accomplish more valuable than the "good enough" that fills my dog's bowl and satisfies his thirst? How would you describe your life, your testimonies, and your experiences? How do you feel right now?

You purchased this book because you want more. You want something better, to be at your best or accomplish something great. It could be improving an area of your personal life into a better relationship or better home life. It could be a better career or greater success as a business owner. You could be an athlete, a writer, dancer, student, mother or father and you want your life and experiences to yield better, best and greater results than it does today. I know that's you, so keep reading.

Defining Greatness

"Greatness is striving for Greatness. It's the ability to consistently put forth your best physical, mental and emotional effort without regard to your circumstance or your ability. Reflect on your life and the mindset of a quitter vs. a conqueror. Which are you?"

How do you go from good to better and then transition into greatness?

Greatness has more to do with continually striving to get better than it does with reaching a certain level of achievement. You can be great once, but that isn't greatness. It's important to note that your greatness is not to be measured in terms of how much you accomplish or do compared to others. Greatness is consistently putting forth your best effort and doing better and better over time.

If you look up greatness in the dictionary, you will see a picture of Carol Johnston. Carol was a gymnast that reached the pinnacle of her craft when at 19 she became a collegiate gymnastics champion. She was also featured in Disney's 1980 TV film "Lefty."

She competed four seasons with the Titans at Cal State Fullerton from 1977-1980. As a Fullerton Titan, Carol became Western Collegiate Athletic Association conference champion on the balance beam in 1977, runner-up in the NCAA meet at Seattle, on both beam and floor, in 1978, and was two-time-All-American as awarded by the Association for Intercollegiate Athletics for Women on balance beam and floor exercise. Also in the first three seasons in which she competed for the Titans, the Cal State Fullerton gymnastics squad compiled a record of 45-0 in meets.

She was the epitome of greatness even though she did not win an Olympic medal. There are countless others who have won Olympic medals, but none as great. Why do I say this?

Carol Johnston was born without a right arm below her elbow. I was a personal witness to this, as I was also a student and Cal State Fullerton during the time she was there. I remember walking through the upper level in the gym and saw this young lady doing flips, and all kinds of complicated gymnastic moves on the balance beam and uneven bars. It was incredible to watch her so gracefully, with only one arm, perform these beautiful fluid movements that other gymnasts could only dream of making.

I can imagine Carol as a young girl watching the Olympics and saying to herself, "I'm going to do that one day. Look, mommy, can you sign me up for gymnastics?" Imagine the drive, courage, dedication and sheer will it took for this little one-arm girl to dream that big. You also have to understand that she didn't do this by herself. She was surrounded by a team that supported, encouraged, mentored and believed in her. She has a great story and I would encourage you to watch the movie. It's very inspiring.

In this chapter, we are defining greatness and showing what it looks like, so when you look in the mirror, you'll understand if you have settled for "good enough" or if you are truly striving for greatness. Don't compare your achievements to the achievements of others. Compare your efforts to efforts of others, their tenacity, their drive and their not settling for "good enough." Carol Johnston says that she was born with drive due to her disability, and never felt sorry for herself. Don't feel sorry for yourself either.

No matter your walk of life, you will have the choice to be great or not. It's a want and a desire that you have to cultivate; an inner drive that you have to feed. You have to choose it. Consider the following examples and reflect on them from the mindset of a quitter compared to a conqueror.

Student -- A student earning a B or C can be a great student. An A student may not. Being a great student means you have good citizenship in class, you turn in all of your homework, you respect the teacher and you study for your tests. The greatest element in this progression is that you continue to learn and obtain a better understanding of each subject you take. A great student gets better by consistently applying better and better study habits.

An A student may be arrogant, act up in class, not respect the teacher and just have a natural gift of understanding in that particular subject area. They test well and get their A without being a great student.

> *"Greatness transcends what you are trying to accomplish and becomes who you are as a person."*

Husband/Wife -- You can be a good husband or good wife and not have a good marriage. First of all, there are two levels higher than good. They are best and great. If you strive to be good and aren't striving to consistently improve your relationship to make it better and ultimately into the best relationship you've ever had, you're really saying "what I'm doing in our marriage today is good enough. This is all you're going to get from me."

Really? How many of you would say that to your wife or husband or the person you are engaged to?

There are two big questions that arise out of this and it applies to all of your relationships; work, friends, family, etc.

1. If your stance is "what I'm doing in this relationship today is good enough," what does that say about how you really feel about your partner? Are they not worth receiving your best or greatest efforts to ensure the relationship continues to grow and strengthen?

2. Why are you not giving your best? Why are you stopping short of working to make things better?

If you are one who wants more, you first need to learn how to do something better in the relationship. You could be a better listener, a better helper around the house, get better at not holding a grudge, better at forgiving, better at sharing, better at holding a conversation or better at being open and vulnerable with your spouse. The list goes on and on.

23

You can have a great relationship by simply putting forth the effort to make things better and not settling for what your efforts currently yield. The strongest bonds in relationships are forged through trials because you go through it together building trust and commitment as you see it through. The simple fact that you put forth an effort to make things better shows you value the other person and that they and their well-being are truly important to you.

Business Owner, Employee or Manager -- An employee earning $35,000 per year can be a great employee, whereas, someone who makes $200,000 per year may not. The same goes for business owners. A small business may be a great business compared to a mid-size business that has 10,000 employees with global customers. Money is most often used to measure success and it's a very poor metric for several reasons.

Reflect on this statement, "money can't buy happiness." I've worked for large and small companies and by and far; the smaller ones tend to be more like family and maintain a higher level of happiness among the employees.

Many think the measure of a company's greatness rises in comparison to its size. "They make a lot of money and have over 5,000 employees. They are doing a great job over there at ACME Corp."

I worked with a Fortune 100 company as a consultant where I made a high wage and most of the employees were paid very well. It was a great place to work, had a great atmosphere and had great working relationships between the departments.

Well, not really. The money was great, but I hated going there. It was not a great place to work because each day, the odds of you hearing someone being cursed out or having someone curse at you were 100%. There was a lot of tension between IT and Finance to the point where VP's would curse each other during conference calls. I'm talking about the F-bomb variety in terms of choice words.

The departments didn't work well together because they each wanted credit for the project's success and thus they sought how to either make their department look better or the other one to look worse.

They were like the spouse who says, "my behavior is good enough," but there was room to get better. Our project management team worked hard to build rapport and forge better relationships between departments. We encouraged better collaboration and more honest reporting where everyone could get credit for success. The result was, we became a better team over time and delivered a successful project where everyone received their due credit.

Athlete -- An athlete who runs the 40-yard dash in 4.6 seconds can be a great football or baseball player compared to someone who can run a 4.3 and can't catch, throw or hit. In sports, it's just that simple. An athlete may test good for speed, but if they can't handle pressure, don't work on the little things that perfect their technic, hand-eye coordination and balance, they won't improve and thus will never be great. Athletes who physically train consistently and who become a "student of the game" mentally, continue to get better and improve their performance.

The thing about sports is that you don't have to be great in everything, but you do have to improve. In most sports, there are 4-5 key areas that truly measure how good you are.

In baseball, it's hit, hit for power, run the bases, catch and throw. You don't have to excel in all of those areas to be great. You can excel in one or two and be considered a great baseball player. You adapt to change, identify weaknesses and work to get better and better to cement your greatness and become a "complete ballplayer."

In football, it's straight-line speed as in the 40-yard dash that is the gold standard, but it's not the best measurement of greatness for football. For track, yes. For football, no. The better test is how well you maintain speed when changing direction and coming out of breaks, you are also tested for strength, jumping ability, catching, throwing and tackling. So, you see, there is a whole set of attributes that you can improve upon. Collectively, your continual improvement in these complementary areas results in you getting better and better, and eventually achieving greatness.

Like everything else, we sometimes measure a single piece of data and not the collective data points that give a clearer picture of how something can or is getting better or measured for greatness. In sports and in life, there are so many intangibles to what makes someone great and many ways to measure it.

Intangibles are mostly personal and related to how you feel and perform. See if you can answer "Yes" to all of the following questions:

- Do you handle pressure well?
- Can you perform when you are upset?
- Are you secure enough to say, "I don't understand, when everyone else does?"
- Can you make what you know is the right decision regardless of what other people may think about it?

- Do you demonstrate a sense of urgency when it's sorely needed?
- Can you motivate yourself?
- Can you do an honest critique of yourself and listen to others?
- Do you want to be great?

Your Personal Greatness – As a sports coach, I teach a concept in basketball that challenges my players to think ahead as they play. I want them to develop options for the future in real-time, based on what has yet to take place. In other words, act or make decisions while factoring in future assumptions.

In basketball, A good player can think one pass ahead and will have two options in their head for what they could do before they even get the ball. It works the same with someone who plays chess. Think ahead. I explain to my players that one of the differences between high school, college and professional basketball players is the ability to anticipate. This ability to think ahead is a key component to successfully transition from Good to Best to Great.

This will work in every aspect of your life. It works with business, relationships, personal and professional goals, sports and anything else you can think of. You have to think and plan ahead, then be able to pivot and adjust to unforeseen happenings.

In this book, we explore the concept of going from good to great. We'll get more into it in the next chapter and it goes like this:

Good → Better1 → **Best** → Better2 → **Great**

Now, let's get back to basketball. **Good** basketball players can think of 2 options for what they are going to do before the ball is passed to them. They survey the floor and anticipate what the defense will do. If the defense comes up fast, they'll dribble around them and then shot or pass to a teammate. If the defense lays off, they'll shoot.

A **Better** basketball player can think of 3 or 4 options for what they are going to do before the ball is passed to them and they also anticipate what the teammate they are passing to will do before they pass it to them.

The **Better** player surveys the floor and anticipates what the defense will do. If they come up fast, they'll dribble around them and then shot or pass to one of 2 teammates, whichever one is more open and has a better shot.

The **Best** players do the same things, but they have 5 or more options in their head before the ball gets to them. They survey the floor and have options for getting the ball to all of the other 4 teammates. They anticipate who will have the better shot or a better opportunity to pass to a third teammate who will take the shot 2 or more passes in the future.

All of this is done before they get the ball. For each of the options to pass to another teammate, there are contingencies based on what the defense does. As they execute, they are making several decisions as they run, dribble and position their bodies for the next move.

What separates the **Great** players from the **Best** is that **Great** players are more consistent in choosing the correct option, making the correct pass, taking the correct shot and executing the pass and making the shot at a much higher rate. They do this no matter their ability or circumstance. They read their teammates and understand that they will be a recipient of a pass, 2 or 3 passes from now, so they immediately move to the correct position on the floor while those future passes are delivered. This is what is measured as "game speed". Game speed is always faster and more effective than physical speed.

Have you seen a great team and it seems like they all know what the other one is thinking? Not all are great athletes as far as jumping or quickness, but they all seem to move faster than the other team. This is that "game speed." This is where a player with less athleticism executes a play just as fast or faster than a defensive player who is faster and more athletic. This also applies on the defensive side of the ball. This is an effective attribute for all sports, business owners, employees, managers and all types of relationships.

Anticipate how what you say and do now will impact your future and make your decisions based on that. If I know what's going to happen 2 passes in the future, I decide now to get in position to benefit from that knowledge. While the defense is reacting to now, I am reacting to the future. By consistently applying this concept, I and my teammates are able to play faster than the other team and be in a position to either score or defend by the time they figure out what we are doing.

In a relationship, you can avoid so many mistakes like the slip of the tongue when you say something you don't mean. You can't un-say something. You don't always get an opportunity to undo what you've done, but maybe if you had taken a little look into the future you could have made a better decision. Looking forward leads to better decisions. Thus, you become a better decision maker, and you start making your best decisions. Add consistency and you will become a great decision maker.

It may sound like something Captain Obvious would say. But the result of thinking ahead yields nothing but good results. You don't have to be number one in the category you are being measured in. You are great if you record your measurement and continue to work on improving and getting better. As you improve, stop, measure and see where you can make further improvements. Then continue the process of bettering yourself.

In business, we call this Strategic Planning. You develop a multi-year plan designed to provide a roadmap to help a company get from A to Z. The plan has actionable tasks designed to help the company reach the objectives and goals outlined in the plan.

There are also contingencies for price changes, market demand, changes in the economy, staff reductions and other events that allow the company to adapt and adjust to stay on track to meet their objectives.

These businesses don't have to be number one in their industry, they just need to constantly improve in how they go to market, treat their employees and manage growth. A company that does this is a great company to work for and invest in.

Likewise, your greatness doesn't mean you have to have the top mark, a perfect marriage, the best job, the most strength, the most stamina or the best speed or jumping ability.

Achieving greatness means you recognize there is room for improvement. Greatness is a by-product of repeating the process of getting better. It also helps to have a plan.

Your marriage, job, business, achievements, relationships, health, spirituality and results can all be better. Good wants you settle for how good you are today. Good doesn't look into the future. It wants you to quit and move onto something else. Good will invoke your emotions and influence you into making bad decisions.

Achieving Greatness

*"If you only strive to be good or put
forth a good effort, you'll always fall
short of being great."*

You can and will achieve greatness within
your own capabilities by measuring it relative
to your previous progress. This is where you
are able to sustain great efforts. You
consistently apply your best effort and do not
settle for good enough. We'll show you how.

There are four levels to reaching greatness.
They are good, better, best and great. Better
being the most important because it moves
between all the levels.

Good → Better1 → **Best** → Better2 → **Great**

On a difficult test, your grade is a C. That's
good because you didn't fail, but you could
have done better and received a B if you had
studied more diligently. If you had studied
with friends or a tutor and turned in all of
your homework, this extra effort could have
helped you grasp all of the information needed
to score the best grade, which is an A.

34

If you consistently get A's, you're a great student, right? No. If you consistently get better grades you are a great student. Between best and great is better. You have to consistently do better to become great.

A key to this process is recognizing that greatness is relative to your capability, and shouldn't be measured by a universal standard. So, don't compare yourself to anyone else. Measure to see if you are consistently doing better yourself. That is what will lead you to greatness.

We all have our unique talents and abilities. Most students are not great in both Math and English. It's usually one or the other.

Some students may have difficulty with a subject and no matter how much effort they put forth, they will never get an A and this is OK. They can, however, achieve their best result consistently, even if that is a B or C. They are still a great student because they are striving to be great by consistently working to get better.

This applies to life as well. We can't all be rocket scientists, professional athletes or millionaire businessmen, but we can all strive and achieve better results in everything we do within our potential and capability. Over time we become great in the areas we operate in by consistently getting better and by leveraging our strengths.

Two of my favorite basketball players of all time are Magic Johnson and Larry Bird. They both were less athletic than most of their opponents, as far as speed and jumping, yet they were voted in as two of the top 5 all-time NBA's greatest players.

They didn't have the best speed, quickness or jumping ability, but they consistently strived for better results through training, nutrition, studying, preparation and repeated execution. They also thought further into the future on the court than did their peers. This kept them one step ahead of their opponents. We'll touch on the power of developing options and making decisions now based on future events a little later. It's powerful indeed, but let's get back to the different levels leading to greatness.

- **Good** is a level below what you are capable of. It's an average effort or result. It's good compared to what you're capable of, but not your best.

- **Better1** is raising your good to the Best level. You don't settle at Good and won't settle for anything less than a Personal Best. You have still had yet to reach your full potential even though this is a

Personal Best.

- **Best** is hitting your peak performance at a point in time, in that specific moment.

- **Better 2** is not settling after hitting a Personal Best. You treat your Personal Best like a Good and work to become even Better.

- **Great** is being able to put forth a Better2 or Best effort and result consistently over time, no matter your circumstance or your ability. Consistently performing at this level equates to greatness.

Here is the process in a nutshell. Repeat this over and over and you'll yield consistent growth and great results. For the areas in your life that you want to move from good to great, do the following:

1. *Start with Greatness as your goal. Don't stop at Good Enough.*

2. *Work hard toward achieving a Better1 result or personal Best. You can, because you are capable of far more and far more consistency than you realize.*

3. *Turn Good into Better1, then Better1 into a Best.*

4. *Make your Best a Better2 and maintain this level over time. Better2 will naturally move you to the Great level. Focus on remaining at Better2*

5. *Repeat Step 4 to create consistency. This is Greatness.*

Making a difficult shot under pressure doesn't make a ballplayer great. Making that difficult shot consistently under those circumstances and within that ability does. Their desire motivates them. Their effort and familiarity with the situation allow them to excel no matter the circumstance. Preparation and consistency are the keys to their success because they've been in that situation several times before.

Kobe Bryant of the Los Angeles Lakers would regularly spend several hours before and after practice working on taking game-winning shots. He consistently put himself in game-winning situations and circumstances during practice so that when he faced it in a real game, he would be comfortable with his options and responsibility. He was confident he could make that 20-footer from the corner, that 3-pointer from the top of the key or that hard drive to the basket as the clock was winding down because he'd taken those shots and made those moves a thousand times before in practice.

He created consistency through practice to prepare himself for real game situations. Those weren't lucky shots he made at the buzzer, they were regular shots he made a thousand times before in practice. He created a new normal. His normal was great.

Preparation and consistency prepares you for adversity, whether it's from within or from an outside source. To be Great, you have to fight through mental and emotional blocks to stay positive and not settle for "this is good enough." You need a team to help you with this and you can't be afraid to take a shot.

The Fear Factor

"The Israelites saw Goliath and said, 'He is way too big for us to fight. David saw Goliath and said, 'Wow, that guy is big, there's no way I can miss.'"

Fear will come at you in two ways. It either pushes you off track so you move on to something else or it pushes you back to keep you from progressing.

It plays a big part in influencing your decision to label something as "good enough" or not. Fear is an emotion and you should never make a decision or categorization based on emotional impulses or fear. Too many bad decisions have been made based on how we felt at that time. I don't need to give examples because I'm sure you already have some of your own.

You can't un-say something. There are many things we do in the heat of the moment that we regret later. They cannot be undone. There is no reset button in life, so never make a decision when emotions are high. Try to calm down and reset, then make your final decision when you can clearly think through and consider your options.

Our friends at Dictionary.com describe fear in this way:

> Noun. - a distressing emotion aroused by impending danger, evil, pain, etc., whether the threat is real or imagined; anticipation of the possibility that something unpleasant will occur.

Fear is designed to make you doubt yourself, keep you in a certain place and limit the progression to your next level of achievement. Fear is not from God and giving in to fear can make you quit and give up on something that isn't finished or yet perfected. You categorize it as "good enough" and leave it as-is, even though the performance, the quality or quantity could have been improved upon. It wasn't your best performance, or of the best quality, but you stopped before it reached another level. You could be "this close" to reaching your goal and you stop short of what your capable of; short of your potential because you're afraid of something that may not matter, or worse yet, something imagined.

Fear is sometimes disguised in the form of comfort or contentment. We are afraid to try something new, be it leaving a job, starting a relationship, leaving a relationship or making business decisions because we are content with the present results or status. We are content to continue operating under the status quo.

Instead of surrendering to fear, use it as a motivator and reach that next level. Go into "survival mode" and keep pushing forward. Do not stop. Fear means you are close. Close to what?

- Close to a breakthrough
- Close to a new personal best
- Close to accomplishing something new
- Close to overcoming a barrier
- Close to reaching a new level
- Close to becoming great

How many times have you said, "Maybe this isn't for me" or "I tried that before." When you say this, you're telling your audience that you failed and you're not going to try it again. You won't go forward with improving or getting better. "This is good enough so I'm staying right here" or "I'm moving onto something else."

The biggest fear of them all is being the only one in the room that needs help or has a question. All of us have that fear. How many classrooms or meetings have you been in and didn't raise your hand to ask a question about something you didn't understand? By your inaction, you are really saying, "I'm ok without knowing that vital information and I'm good with making a decision or determination based on not knowing everything."

The answer to your questions are only as far away as the time it takes to ask the question. So, ask the question. Embrace fear and get excited because in that moment you are removing that roadblock in your progression from good to great.

Fear can be the energy you need to get past old feelings, overcome doubt, break through and achieve something incredible in your life. Embrace it and move forward.

Next, you'll build a team that will support, encourage, constructively criticize, motivate, manage expectations and help you through all of your barriers as you reach your potential, reach your greatness.

Defining Your Team

"Great things are never done by one person alone. They are done by a team of people. Even Jesus had a team."

A plant requires specific things to grow healthy and mature. It needs soil, water, air, sunlight, and nutrients. Each element needed by the plant serves a purpose. Some provide multiple benefits. These elements collectively provide nutrients, stability and act as catalysts for chemical reactions that promote growth and maturity.

Plants also thrive when exposed to a little fertilizer. So, you might have to go through some stuff that will, in the end, help you grow. You'll struggle, things will go wrong, people may turn on you but you still have to show up every day and perform in the midst of all that stuff to grow into your greatness.

Watch how green your grass grows, how beautiful your flowers become and how bountiful the produce you reap from your garden when it is exposed to a measured amount of fertilizer. Too much fertilizer can damage a plant, but the cultivator, your mentor, can quickly remedy that situation when necessary.

Plants have an organic support system, a team of elements which together comprise a perfect environment for healthy plant growth. To maintain consistency, you'll need a support system as well.

The most successful people in the world all have support systems. You won't be able to find one person that has reached greatness without one. Remember, greatness is not being the greatest, it's performing and producing better and better results consistently over time within your capability and potential.

To maintain consistency and become great, you need people in your corner who will help you break through barriers, keep you going when you want to quit and who provide knowledge, insight and a retrospective of who you are and where you are during this process.

As a project manager, working on a multimillion-dollar software implementation, I managed a team of 15 consultants made up of developers, business analysts, system architects and a scrum master. My team was part of a much larger team of approximately 80-100 people and faced many challenges in

45

delivering our work, managing expectations, dealing with change and navigating the politics in a complex business culture.

I came on board 18 months after the project initially started and had the difficult job of quickly getting up to speed so I could help my team deliver and make the project a success. By the way, when I arrived, the project was over budget and was way overdue. On top of that, there were 3 or 4 project managers before me that couldn't make it work and either quit or were fired. There was a lot of pressure and expectation to start moving things in a more positive direction.

I got off to a rough start and was barely staying above water. I won't go into details, but delivery was not good, we were making mistakes and we weren't hitting our due dates, which lead to delays and additional contract negotiations to secure payment for extending the timeline. I wasn't sure I'd be successful there.

I had a meeting with my two superiors and expressed my challenges. They gave me the perfect solution, form a leadership team. I immediately started identifying who should fill these roles, bringing the best value to the project.

Within two days I had identified and invited my cabinet members to our first meeting. It went great. I took one person from each role on my project team. I now had a team of 15 project team members, and a new leadership team of 5 members. I had a system architect, a scrum master, developer, and two business analysts.

My first words to them were in essence, "I want to help you be successful and I need your help to assist me in making better decisions." My job was to make their jobs easier and shield them from the politics so they could focus on their work and deliver a great product.

In turn, the leadership team would apprise me of everything going on that I would not normally be aware of. We agreed to be very honest and transparent with each other and over time we gained each other's trust. They helped me with the following:

- assess the current state of team morale
- apprise me of things we needed to worry about
- identified what needed to be proactively addressed
- determined how we could deliver better
- share how I could be a better support for them
- identify who was struggling and how to help them

47

- a better way to approach testing issues
- better ways to report our status
- who to include on special assignments

I kept my promise of keeping them out of the politics, kept the client out of their hair, and created a productive environment in which they only had to concentrate on their work and it turned everything around.

I believe the biggest gift I gave them was a voice. I allowed them to speak freely and empowered them to make decisions that we all would be accountable to. Over time some would take the lead in executing the ideas and solutions we came up with that made the project more successful. We became a better team and I became a better project manager and leader.

Forming this leadership group was the best thing we could have done. Everyone on our larger team bought into what we were doing because we were discussing and making decisions together and some of my leaders were leading the charge.

I was able to make better and better decisions and our group came to be highly regarded as the true experts on the project and garnered more respect than had earlier been possible. As a project manager and as a team, we moved from good to better to best and then to a great team. We were now great to work with and the client became more comfortable in relying on us for our expertise, reliability, and quality of work.

So, what about you? How do you start building a team to help you move from good to great?

You have to go back to the plant. It needs soil, water, air, sunlight and nutrients to grow and mature. In the following sections, we'll discuss how each element the plant requires correlates to the makeup of your team.

Let's look at the components of Team Plant and relate them to what will become Team You.

The Plant's Soil provides stability and is a place for the plant to anchor itself and receive nourishment. It's able to establish a root system that absorbs nutrients below ground that gives it stability and health above ground. Your private sessions with your mentor and your team will yield stability, consistency, sustainability, better results, and lead to better decision making in your personal and business life.

Your Soil is your mentor. They provide stability, someone to lean on, learn from, keep you level-headed and on track. They will nurture and guide you.

A mentor is crucial to your progression from good to great. A mentor can enable the mentee to achieve or exceed their life's goals and aspirations, helping them achieve better results and performance. A mentor according to Merriam-Webster is "a trusted counselor and guide."

Depending upon your needs, a mentor shares knowledge and life experiences. Their real-life example shows you what can be done and how to do it. If you anchor yourself to this person, you'll receive a constant flow of valuable "nutrients" that will feed and sustain you as you get better and better on your road to greatness.

Find someone who has accomplished what you are trying to do. At the time of this writing, my son is playing high school football and has a desire to continue playing in college and then the NFL. So, we hired Clint Floyd, a former college and professional football player to help train him. Clint has been where my son wants to go and is a great mentor for him.

His advice and life experiences give my son a broader understanding of what it takes to reach his goals with football and he is learning how to get there through the specialized training and guidance he is receiving.

Who will be your mentor? Find a mentor that is willing to build a relationship with you and who has been where you want to go.

The Plant's Water refreshes and vitalizes bringing forth and sustaining life. A seed can remain dormant for decades, but once you expose it to water it starts to grow. Water gives and sustains life. A plant cannot survive without a regular supply of water.

Your Water is the person who will encourage you and not let you quit. They won't let you quit no matter what. This is the person that has the right thing to say at the right time. When you feel down, they will have a refreshing effect on you and are the catalyst for bringing your dreams and aspirations back to life and sustaining your drive and enthusiasm.

When you are down, who is that one person you can call on to cheer you up? That person is your water.

The Plant's Air is absorbed through the leaves and is vitally needed for the plant to stay alive. Plant leaves use carbon dioxide from the air to make sugars and starches for the plant to use as food. Another part of the plant that needs air is the roots. Plant roots need oxygen to stay healthy and to do their job of gathering water and nutrients for the plant.

Your Air is your inner circle. These are the people who work closely with you in your day to day activities or in the area, you're striving for greatness in. This is a give and take proposition. They provide you with something and you give back something in return. Plants take in the carbon dioxide we produce and use it to make food for itself. In return, it gives off oxygen for us to breathe and live.

In your inner circle, there is at least one person who rallies behind you in just about everything. They are the ones who are there with you every step of the way, helping you get better and better on your way to becoming and accomplishing your goals and aspirations. In your appreciation, you naturally do things to help them in the same way that plants give back to us.

The Plant's Sunlight is its energy source. Plants get energy from light through a process called photosynthesis. Light affects the growth of a plant. Without light, a plant would not be able to produce the energy it needs to grow.

Your Sunlight is your training partner and source of energy. You have a different kind of energy when you work with this person. You don't get tired and together you both accomplish more in less time than a team twice your size ever could. You work in tandem, with trust that the motive is to do a great job and not trying to get sole credit for a job well done. You are always on the same page, sharing the same goals, drive, and ambition.

When there is a ton of work to be done, their presence alone can brighten your day and give you that boost of energy needed to get the job done. This is your right-hand, your workout partner, your teammate and one of your closest friends.

Your next step is to start identifying your team. Some people may fill more than one role or you may have multiple people for some of the roles. One thing I do recommend is identifying your mentor first, then work with your mentor to fill the roles of the remaining members of your all-star team.

See the Appendix for an example of a form to use is defining your team.

Describe your quest for greatness in the form of a target statement. Be specific in stating your goal. I recommend using the following formula, similar to what is used with software development.

Fill in the blanks to complete your personal target statement using this phraseology:

"I want to (be/have)_____, so I can _____."

Here are some sample thoughts to get you started.

- I want to have a great marriage, so I will have a strong and lasting relationship, setting a positive example for my children
- I want to have a great career, so I can support my family and do work I'm passionate about and enjoy

- I want to be a great ballplayer, so I can contribute to my team's success and secure a spot in the starting lineup, while preparing for the next level

- I want to be an exceptional student so I can achieve high grades, graduate on time, and succeed in both college and life

- I want to be a great business owner, so I can provide well for my family, create job opportunities in the community, and leaving a lasting legacy for my children

- I want to be a great manager, so I can help my employees improve in their roles and provide them a positive work environment

- I want to be a great writer, so I can deliver impactful content in books and articles that positively impact people's lives

- I want to be a great artist, so I can translate the beauty within my mind into visual creations for others to experience and enjoy

- I want to be a great dancer, so I can share my interpretations of music and the joy of dance with others

- I want to be a top-notch real estate professional, so I can helping individuals from all backgrounds find their dream home

- I want to be a great ethical salesperson, so I can earn good money while connecting people with the goods and services they need and desire

- I want to be a great conversationalist, so I can be more comfortable talking to both acquaintances and strangers, allowing people to get to know the authentic me

- I want to be a great friend, so I can offer unwavering support, attentive listening, and assistance within my capabilities to those who depend on me

You not only need to know what you want but why you want it. Figure this out, and you are well on your way to being great. You have to have a WHY or you won't be able to sustain your drive and motivation.

Write down your what's and why's on a piece of paper. Say them outloud each day until you get a clear picture of the path you need to take along with the effort you'll have to expend to get there. Then keep repeating them each day until it becomes a part of you.

Let you team know what you are trying to accomplish and they will help you get there. Your team needs to know your what's and why's in order to help you and provide the best possible support in your journey to greatness in that area.

As you build your team, keep these things in mind. In this real world, we live in, you'll find that you may not have a different person for each role. If you do, that's great, but it's not important how many people you have on your team. It's how many roles you can fill that's important, even if those roles are all filled by only one or two people.

So, as you review the team definition on the next page, don't feel like you need to have a different person for each spot on the team. You are filling roles, not trying to find a person for each role.

Defining Your Team

Target Statement:

"I want to (be/have) _____

so, I can _____."

Role	Description
Mentor	They provide stability, someone to lean on, learn from, keep you level-headed and on track. A mentor will nurture and guide you.
Encourager	The person who will encourage you and not let you quit.
Inner Circle	These are the people who work closely with you in the area you're striving for greatness in.
Your Source of Energy	This is your right-hand, your workout partner, your teammate and one of your closest friends. They will literally get you out of bed or out of the house to make sure you are doing something productive.

Wrapping It Up

"You can lead a horse to water, but you can't make him drink. You can give a man a brain, but you can't make him think."

Follow through will be the key to your success. What are you going to do with what you've just read? My challenge to you is to do something great, be great at something and don't settle for "good enough." I can't force you to strive for greatness with the things that are important to you, that responsibility belongs to you and you alone. You should care enough about yourself to want it yourself. I can challenge you though, dare you to be great and hopefully through this book, provide a spark for your inner drive.

Your inner drive is important because your team won't be around you all the time. They will not always know when they are needed. It's important to be open and transparent with them and to not be afraid to pick up the phone say, "Can you help me with...?"

As we talked before, your answer, your breakthrough, and your relief are often only a question or request away? Knowing what to do next is often just a conversation away.

How silly would it be for the plant to not take in water, sunlight or air? The plant is alive because it doesn't deny itself these essential things. Your dreams and aspirations to be great in something will continue to live as long as you don't refuse the help your team is there to give you on a daily basis.

Remember, fear of letting others know you need help or have questions is not part of who you are now. You aren't subject to the fear factor. Use fear as motivation, knowing that you are "this close" toward reaching your goal.

I want you to be tired of being "good enough." Someone once said, "Good Enough Sucks!" It really does, especially if you are capable of much more. Why settle for a slice, when you originally set out to get the whole pie? Well. Don't worry, now your life will be much richer and much more rewarding because you now have a framework to get there.

This is the start of something great in your life. At the very least, be inspired to reach a personal best and accomplish something you never thought possible. Then repeat the process. This is greatness.

It's not very difficult at all to go from good to great. Don't worry about being the greatest. You only have to worry about getting better and better at what you do. If you consistently improve, greatness will happen naturally.

Good → Better1 → **Best** → Better2 → **Great**

The secret is in the better level. This is where improvement takes place, where you transform into a better athlete, better employee, better spouse, better friend, better decision maker, better....

Good is bad and settling for good enough is not an option. You now have a support system and an environment designed to keep you winning. You can't help but get better if you let the system work for you.

Now. Go find a piece of paper and write down what you want to achieve greatness in. Then find a mentor you can build a relationship with, someone who has done what you are trying to do and is willing to work with you and stick it out until the very end.

Next, you need to go out and get your team together. A team that is in alignment with your goals and objectives and who want to see you succeed.

Who is that **encourager** to keep you uplifted and in a positive frame of mind? This is the person who brings you out of the dumps and motivates you. You smile when you think about them or hear their name.

Who is your **inner circle**? Not just anyone that is close, an inner circle that is aware of what you are trying to do and will work alongside you to see it yield better and better results.

Who is your **sunlight**? The one person that you love to work with or can partner with to realize great results. You are able to quickly put things into action and see results much quicker with this person. Work doesn't seem like work with this person. You feed off each other and get things done.

Work within the process and rely on your team, keeping the lines of communication open. There is nothing you can't get better at and therefore your greatness cannot be denied. Review this book as you go through the process of enriching your life until the concepts and definitions are a part of who you are.

You'll be better for it and so will the people who are watching and supporting you. As you progress in this, you'll naturally seek out people to bless with this knowledge as well.

Over time, it becomes easier and easier and before you know it, you've reached a new level of greatness.

Good Enough Sucks!

Don't Suck.

Be GREAT!!!

From the Author... Thank you for taking this journey with me. If you enjoyed this book, please go to Amazon and write your honest review. I would love your feedback on how you or someone you love were helped in their journey to Happiness.

Submit your review here

Tools To Bring It Home

The Definitions

The Process

Target Statement Forms

The Definitions:

- **Good** is a level below what you are capable of. It's an average effort or result.

- **Better1** is raising your good to the Best level. You don't settle at Good and won't settle for anything less than a Personal Best. You have still had yet to reach your full potential even though this is a Personal Best.

- **Best** is hitting your peak performance at a point in time, in that specific moment.

- **Better 2** is not settling after hitting a Personal Best. You treat your Personal Best like a Good and work to become even Better.

- **Great** is being able to put forth a Better2 or Best effort and result consistently over time, no matter your circumstance or your ability. Consistency at this level equates to greatness.

The Process:

Along with studying these definitions, there is a process you must follow to reach a level of greatness. Repeat this over and over and you'll yield consistent growth and results. For the areas in your life that you want to move from Good to Great, do the following:

1. *Start with Greatness as your goal. Don't stop at Good Enough.*

2. *Work hard toward achieving a Better1 result or personal Best. You can, because you are capable of far more and far more consistency than you realize.*

3. *Turn Good into Better1, then Better1 into Best.*

4. *Make your Best a Better2 and maintain this level over time. Better2 will naturally move you to the Great level. Focus on remaining at Better2*

5. *Repeat Step 4 to create consistency. This is Greatness.*

Defining Your Team

Target Statement:

"**I want to (be/have)** _____

_____

so, I can _____."

Role	Description
Mentor	
Encourager	
Inner Circle	
Your Source of Energy	

Defining Your Team

Target Statement:

"I want to (be/have) _____
_____

so, I can _____."

Role	Description
Mentor	
Encourager	
Inner Circle	
Your Source of Energy	

Defining Your Team

Target Statement:

"I want to (be/have) _____
_____

so, I can _____**."**

Role	Description
Mentor	
Encourager	
Inner Circle	
Your Source of Energy	

Defining Your Team

Target Statement:

"I want to (be/have) _____

_____

so, I can _____."

Role	Description
Mentor	
Encourager	
Inner Circle	
Your Source of Energy	

Defining Your Team

Target Statement:

"I want to (be/have) _____

_____

so, I can _____."

Role	Description
Mentor	
Encourager	
Inner Circle	
Your Source of Energy	

Also by the Author

Don't Let The Man In The Mirror Block Your Pursuit Of Happiness is a practical and deeply

authentic guide that aims to help readers break free from self-sabotaging beliefs and dare to achieve true joy. Intertwining spiritual insights, powerful quotes, personal anecdotes, and honest advice that encourages you to reflect on your life choices, this book challenges you to break the cycle of happiness destroying behavior, shatter inauthenticity, and build an unbreakable foundation for lasting happiness.

With a rich collection of lessons focused on honesty, openness, integrity, and faith, readers will learn how to transform their personal relationships, start standing up for their beliefs, and stop ignoring how they really feel. *Don't Let The Man In The Mirror Block Your Pursuit Of Happiness* is a must-read for anyone who feels like they're not being true to themselves.

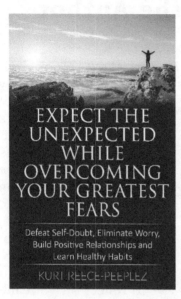

Learn to eliminate your fears within minutes of reading this book! Every fear can be overcome. First, you have to examine your fears and not just ride the emotion. Upon further review, you'll find that most if not all your fears are manageable, and you will be able to negotiate outcomes.

I've faced many fears in my life and have found through my own experience and of those around me that we have nothing to be afraid of. When you apply knowledge and understanding to your circumstance, fear becomes an option.

This book will teach you how to turn your fears into options that you can implement to make your life better. Get ready to eliminate worry, defeat, and self-doubt. Learn how to build healthy habits. Enjoy this book and live your life full of options and free of fear.

It's a fact we all need deliverance from something. No one is on the same level as God and this is what it is all about. We are to be Holy as He is Holy, but we are imperfect. There are many things that can hinder our spiritual growth. Most of those hindrances are hidden. They can be little things, such as the 101 in the list you've read. The point is to look at ourselves in the mirror. Look for things we may have overlooked in the past that are slowing us down spiritually in the present. We need to be delivered from them to maintain our spiritual momentum and strength.

In the book, Letters In Search of Deliverance, Author and Minister, Kurt Reece-Peeplez helps us understand that we are like letters who are delivered to various places determined by how we are addressed. If it has the correct address, a letter will be delivered to the intended destination. If it has the wrong address, the letter will be delivered to the wrong place. If there is no return address, the letter may get lost or destroyed. The way you address your situations determine how successful your deliverance from them will be.

Read this book and you will:

- Find the energy to grow Spiritually Stronger

- Get the Spiritual Deliverance you are seeking.

- Determine where you are Spiritually.

- Feed your Spirit more than you Feed your Flesh.

- Obtain a complete Deliverance.

- Strengthen your Spiritual Foundation.

- Maintain your delivered state by looking to Jesus

"It all boils down to how you address your situations." Filled with several scriptural references and two simple exercises, this book helps you develop a personal plan for deliverance that really works.

Appendix

Notes

Appendix

Made in the USA
Las Vegas, NV
16 December 2023

82961890R00049